Sports Illustrated KIDS

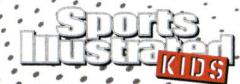

RONALDO CHOPS AND SHIRT SWAPS

FOOTBALL'S GREATEST SIGNATURE MOVES, CELEBRATIONS AND MORE

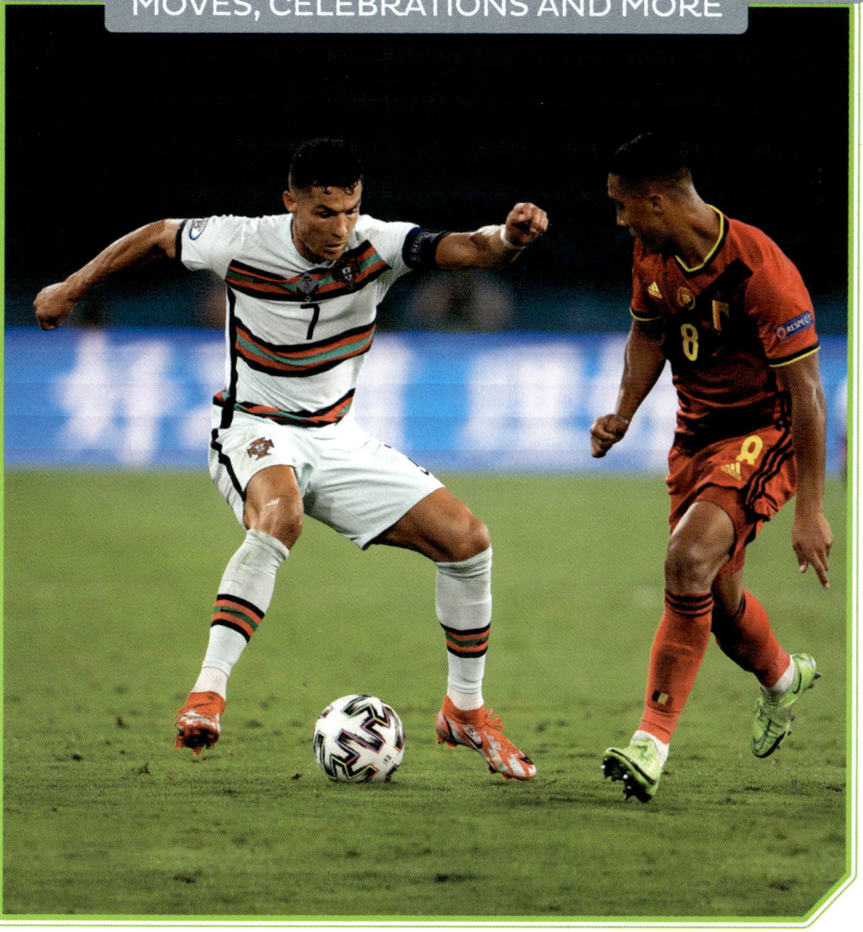

by Steve Foxe

raintree
a Capstone company — publishers for children

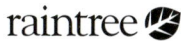

Raintree is an imprint of Capstone Global Library Limited, a company incorporated in England and Wales having its registered office at 264 Banbury Road, Oxford, OX2 7DY – Registered company number: 6695582

www.raintree.co.uk
myorders@raintree.co.uk

Copyright © Capstone Global Library Limited 2025

The moral rights of the proprietor have been asserted. All rights reserved. No part of this publication may be reproduced in any form or by any means (including photocopying or storing it in any medium by electronic means and whether or not transiently or incidentally to some other use of this publication) without the written permission of the copyright owner, except in accordance with the provisions of the Copyright, Designs and Patents Act 1988 or under the terms of a licence issued by the Copyright Licensing Agency, 5th Floor, Shackleton House, 4 Battle Bridge Lane, London, SE1 2HX (www.cla.co.uk). Applications for the copyright owner's written permission should be addressed to the publisher.

ISBN: 978 1 3982 5759 7

Editorial Credits
Editor: Donald Lemke; Designer: Kayla Rossow; Media Researcher: Svetlana Zhurkin; Production Specialist: Katy LaVigne

Printed and bound in India

Image Credits
Associated Press: Pool/Thanassis Stavrakis, cover, 1; Getty Images: AFP/Franck Fife, 21, AFP/Lionel Bonaventure, 23, Dan Istitene, 9, Denis Doyle, 14, 17, Elsa, 5, Gonzalo Arroyo Moreno, 16, Jed Jacobsohn, 25, Juan Manuel Serrano Arce, 15, Julian Finney, 4 (bottom), Keystone, 11, Rick Stewart, 19, Valerio Pennicino, 18; Newscom: Action Plus/John Patrick Fletcher, 13, Mirrorpix/John Varley, 29; Shutterstock: Alexander_P, 8 and throughout, Alexey Seleykov (soccer ball), cover, 1, DarkPlatypus (dotted wave), back cover and throughout, GelgelNasution (soccer player), 4 (top) and throughout; Sports Illustrated: Jerry Cooke, 7, Robert Beck, 26, 27

British Library Cataloguing in Publication Data
A full catalogue record for this book is available from the British Library.

CONTENTS

Signature football 4
Playing hooky 6
Turn it up! 10
Get the chop 14
Faking it! 18
Strike a pose 20
Shirts vs skins 24
A different kind of trophy 28

Glossary 30
Find out more 31
Index 32
About the author 32

Words in **bold** are in the glossary.

SIGNATURE FOOTBALL

Football is a sport enjoyed around the world. It is filled with dazzling kicks, last-minute goals and thrilling wins.

Players for Argentina and France compete during the 2022 FIFA World Cup.

Megan Rapinoe celebrates after scoring a goal.

Some football moves and celebrations are extra special. They're one-of-a-kind, **famous** with fans or impossible to stop. They are often called football's greatest **signature** moves.

PLAYING HOOKY

Edson Arantes do Nascimento, better known as Pelé, is often called the greatest football player of all time. The International Olympic Committee named him Athlete of the Century in 1999. Early in his career, Pelé helped to turn a simple kick into one of the game's greatest signature moves.

> Pelé won his first World Cup at the age of 17 when he played for Brazil in 1958.

Pelé playing for the New York Cosmos in 1975

The kick that Pelé made famous is called the **rabona**. This name comes from a Spanish word meaning "playing hooky".

To perform the kick, a player plants one foot close to the ball. They swing their other leg behind their planted leg. Then, the player kicks the ball with their legs crossed!

PELÉ'S WORLD CUP STATS

Games Played: 14
Goals: 12
Championships: 3

Barcelona's Neymar Júnior (right) performs a rabona kick.

Pelé didn't create the rabona kick. But he was one of the first players to have it recorded on video. After seeing Pelé do it, more players started using this effective kick.

TURN IT UP!

Dutch sports hero Johan Cruyff is one of football's all-time legends. After he stopped playing, Cruyff became a successful coach and manager in the sport as well.

Cruyff played for the Netherlands national team and helped them to reach the World Cup final in 1974.

Johan Cruyff plays against Uruguay in 1974.

During his playing days, Cruyff perfected a move that still carries his name. It is known as the "Cruyff turn".

Cruyff knew that one of the most important skills in football is keeping control of the ball. The Cruyff turn allows a player to completely change direction if the other team is blocking them.

With one leg next to the ball, Cruyff would use the other to kick the ball straight behind him. Cruyff would then turn around sharply to drive the ball back and around the opposing team.

Arsenal's Francis Coquelin performs a Cruyff turn.

GET THE CHOP

Portugal's Cristiano Ronaldo has won dozens of trophies. He has been given the European Golden Boot award four times.

That's more than any other player in Europe! When Ronaldo scores a goal, he often jumps and shouts, "Siiiuuu!" (meaning "Yes!). It's his signature celebration.

But there's another move that's named after him: the "Ronaldo chop".

To perform his famous chop, Ronaldo leaps in front of the ball. He kicks it at an angle using the inside of his strong foot.

Ronaldo prepares to chop the ball with the inside of his right foot.

This helps him change direction quickly. It confuses the other team. Ronaldo uses his other foot to protect the ball from being taken away.

FAKING IT!

The Elastico is another signature football move – and a **tricky** one. The move was made famous by two-time FIFA World Player of the Year, Ronaldinho.

The move involves kicking the ball away using the outside of the boot and then quickly kicking it back with the inside of the boot. It can fool defenders and help with dribbling. It's a strong move on the pitch!

STRIKE A POSE

American Megan Rapinoe is one of the most awarded women in football. In 2019, she also gave the sport one of its biggest viral moments.

After scoring two goals against France in the Women's World Cup quarter-final match, Rapinoe **posed** with her arms up and a grin on her face.

Megan Rapinoe poses at the 2019 Women's World Cup.

Photos of this victory pose quickly spread across social media. It inspired **memes** and many comments.

Rapinoe is known for her **confidence** on and off the pitch. It's no surprise that photos of the pose took off!

SHIRTS VS SKINS

It's common for male players to rip off their shirts in celebration of scoring a goal or winning a game. But in 1999, US women's football player Brandi Chastain caused a stir when she did the same.

After scoring a penalty kick against China in the final round of the Women's World Cup, Chastain took off her shirt. She spun it around her head before dropping to her knees. Some people believed it was wrong for a woman football player to celebrate this way. Others loved it!

Sports Illustrated featured Chastain on the cover in July 1999.

Chastain stood by her decision. The photos of her celebrating her winning goal ended up on the covers of lots of magazines. They inspired girls around the world.

A Different Kind of Trophy

One of the greatest signs of respect between athletes is swapping shirts after a game. Although taking someone else's sweaty clothes might sound gross, it's a way to remember a hard-fought game.

The tradition is at least 100 years old. One of the most memorable shirt swaps was in 1970. Football legends Pelé and Bobby Moore swapped shirts after their teams, Brazil and England, faced each other in the World Cup.

Pelé and Moore swap shirts at the World Cup in 1970.

GLOSSARY

confidence a feeling of certainty

famous well-known or widely recognized

meme a funny or interesting picture or video that is spread widely online especially through social media

pose to strike a specific stance or position, usually to celebrate or express confidence

rabona a football kick where a player swings their stronger foot from behind their other leg to strike the ball with the outside of their boot

signature a distinctive or unique mark, move or style that represents someone

tricky difficult to do or understand, often involving cleverness or deception

FIND OUT MORE

BOOKS

Football's Greatest Moments (Ultimate Football Heroes), Tom Palmer (Dino Books, 2024)

Strikers and Scarves: Behind the Scenes of Match Day Football, Thomas Kingsley Troupe (Raintree, 2024)

The Football School Encyclopedia, Alex Bellos (Walker Books, 2023)

WEBSITES

FIFA: The Home of Football
www.fifa.com/fifaplus/en

Football Facts for Kids
kids.kiddle.co/Football

INDEX

Chastain, Brandi 24–27
Cruyff, Johan 10–12
Cruyff turn 11–12, 13
Elastico 18–19
European Golden Boot award 14
FIFA World Player of the Year 18
International Olympic Committee 6
Moore, Bobby 28, 29
Pelé 6, 7, 8, 9, 28, 29

rabona kick 8–9
Rapinoe, Megan 5, 20–21
Ronaldinho 18–19
Ronaldo chop 15–17
Ronaldo, Cristiano 14–17
shirt swaps 28, 29
Women's World Cup 20, 21, 26
World Cup 4, 6, 8, 10, 20, 21, 26, 28, 29

ABOUT THE AUTHOR

Steve Foxe is the author of over 75 comics and children's books including *X-Men '92: House of XCII*, *Rainbow Bridge*, *Adventure Kingdom* and the Spider-Ham series from Scholastic. He has written for companies such as Pokémon, Mario, LEGO City, Batman, Justice League, Baby Shark and many more.